# MASTER THEORY

## Advanced Harmony & Arranging Workbook

by Charles S. Peters and Paul Yoder

The Sixth Workbook in the MASTER THEORY SERIES

Contents



ISBN 0-8497-0159-7

# ARRANGING FOR VOICES

In learning to write four part choral arrangements ( S A T B ) it is necessary to know the average range of each voice.

The interval between the Soprano-Alto and Alto-Tenor should stay within an octave. The Tenor and Bass parts may be more than an octave apart at times.

ANGELS FROM THE REALMS OF GLORY

* 5th omitted, Root doubled.

Here is an example of a Chorale for four voices in the Key of a minor. Notice the Inversions.

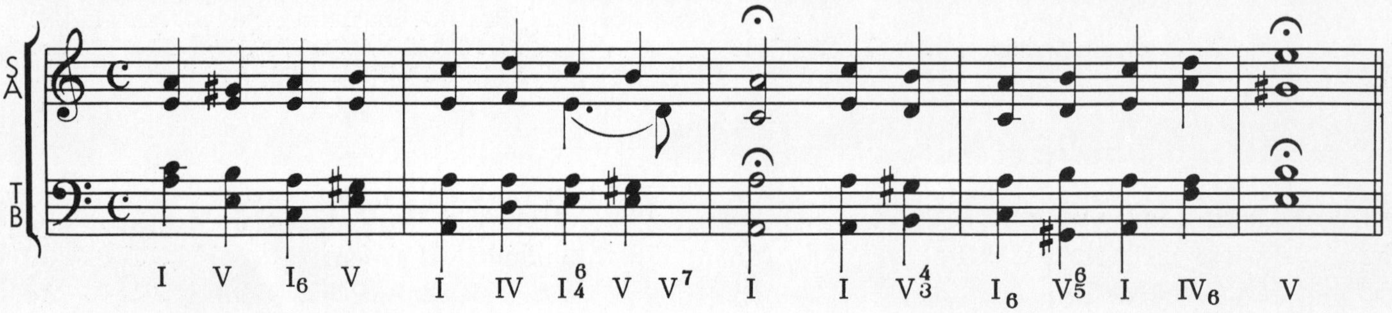


# SECONDARY CHORDS

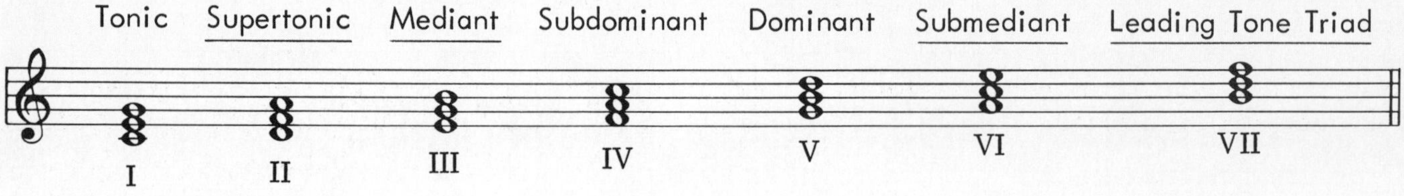


The following example contains all four SECONDARY CHORDS.

WELSH MELODY

# TRANSPOSING INSTRUMENTS

In writing for wind instruments, certain parts must be transposed to other keys. Instruments that sound where the music is written are said to be in CONCERT PITCH. These include: - Piccolo in C - Flute - Oboe - Bassoon - Trombone - Baritone (Bass Clef) - Basses.

## SAXOPHONE QUARTET

Music for the E♭ Alto Saxophone is written a MAJOR SIXTH above the actual sound.

Music for the B♭ Tenor Saxophone is written ONE OCTAVE plus a MAJOR SECOND above the actual sound.

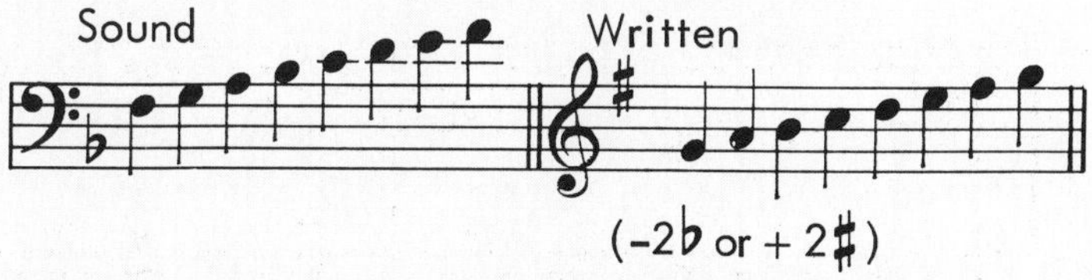


Music for the E♭ Baritone Saxophone is written ONE OCTAVE plus a MAJOR SIXTH above the actual sound.

## BRASS QUARTET

Music for the B♭ Cornet is written a MAJOR SECOND above the actual sound.

Music for the Horn in F is written a PERFECT FIFTH above the actual sound.

Music for the Trombone is written the same as the actual sound.

## CLARINET QUARTET

Music for the B♭ Clarinet is written a MAJOR SECOND above the actual sound.

Music for the E♭ Alto Clarinet is written a MAJOR SIXTH above the actual sound.

Music for the B♭ Bass Clarinet is written ONE OCTAVE and a MAJOR SECOND above the actual sound.

# FORM IN MUSIC

The word FORM is used to describe the fundamental organization of music. The study of FORM concerns the analysis of the basic plan of a musical composition, including the elements of MELODY, RHYTHM AND HARMONY.

In Book 5 of the Master Theory Series (Intermediate Harmony), we analyzed the harmonic structure of numerous hymns and folk songs. To analyze the FORM of these compositions, we must divide them into smaller units such as the PHRASE and the PERIOD.

A PHRASE is a small unit of melody expressing a musical thought. The end of each PHRASE is marked with a comma (,).

Example 1 represents the first PHRASE of this folk song. Notice that it ends with a feeling of temporary repose but not one of finality.

CLEMENTINE

Phrase A

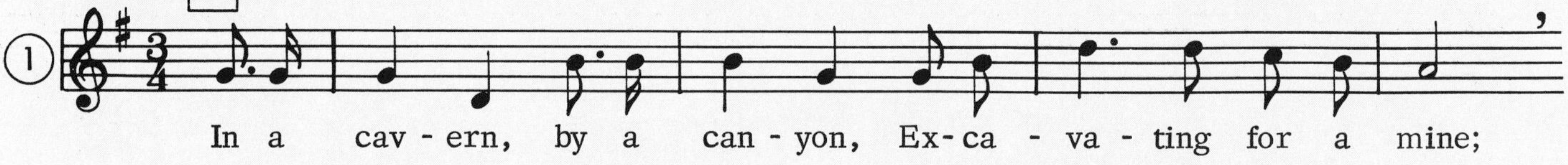


Example 2 shows the second PHRASE of this same song. Notice that the rhythm is exactly the same as that of the first phrase but this second phrase ends with a feeling of completion.

The combination of two phrases, ending with a feeling of finality, is called a PERIOD. The end of each PERIOD is marked with a bracket ].

Phrase B

The third and fourth phrases below (examples 3 and 4) use the same melodic line as the first two phrases. If we call the first phrase A and the second phrase B, we would analyze the form of this song as A-B-A-B. The entire song, consisting of two periods, is known as a DOUBLE PERIOD.

Phrase A

Phrase B

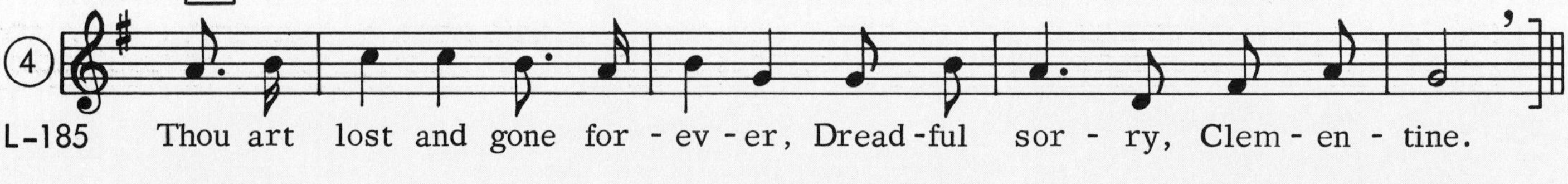

# STUDENT ASSIGNMENT

Date ________

Grade ________

1. Write the entire chorus of "CLEMENTINE" below in the indicated bar lines. Place the proper letter at the beginning of each PHRASE. Place a comma at the end of each PHRASE and a bracket at the end of each PERIOD. Since there are no words here, you may join the dotted eighth and sixteenth notes with a beam as shown. Since this song starts on the 3rd beat, there will be only 2 beats in the last measure.

CLEMENTINE

Montrose

①

2. Write an original melody of sixteen measures in A-B-A-B form. Choose your own key signature and time signature. Make both A phrases exactly alike and both B phrases exactly alike. Mark the phrases and periods as above.

②

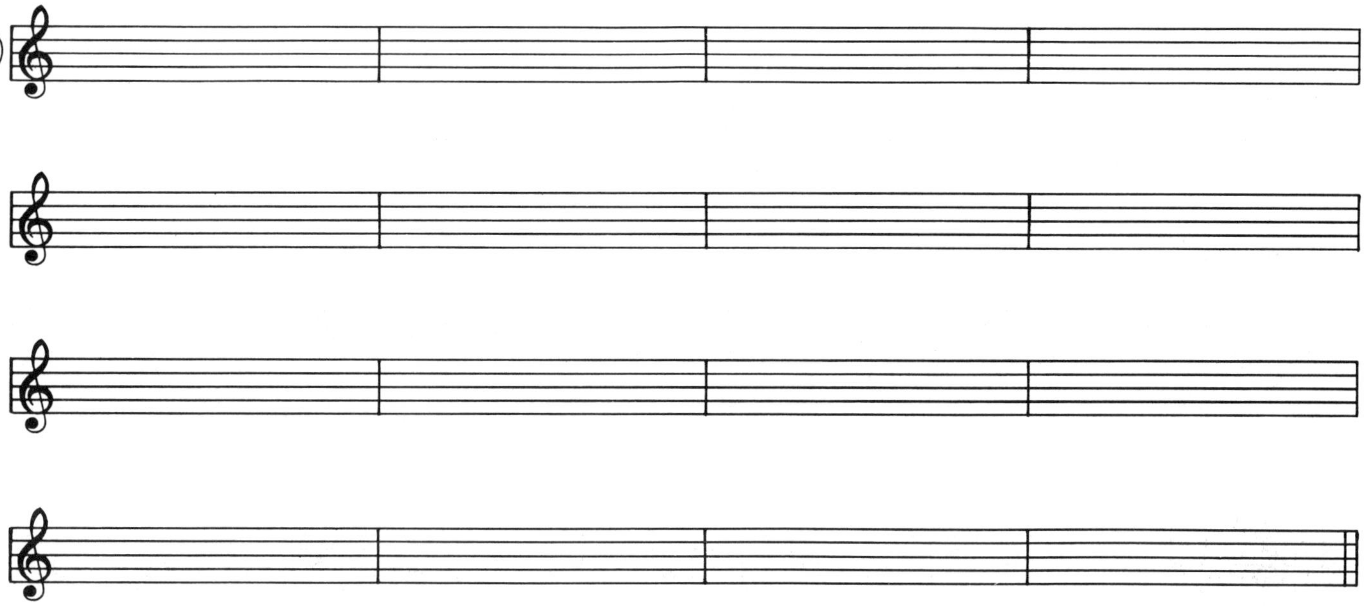

# FORM IN MUSIC (continued)

In many songs and hymns you will find a similarity between phrases but not always an exact duplication. Ex. 1 shows a hymn written in A-B-A-B form in which the two A phrases are exactly alike but there is a slight variation between the two B phrases.
The eighth notes are connected here because they occur on a single syllable.

SOFTLY NOW THE LIGHT OF DAY

C. M. von Weber

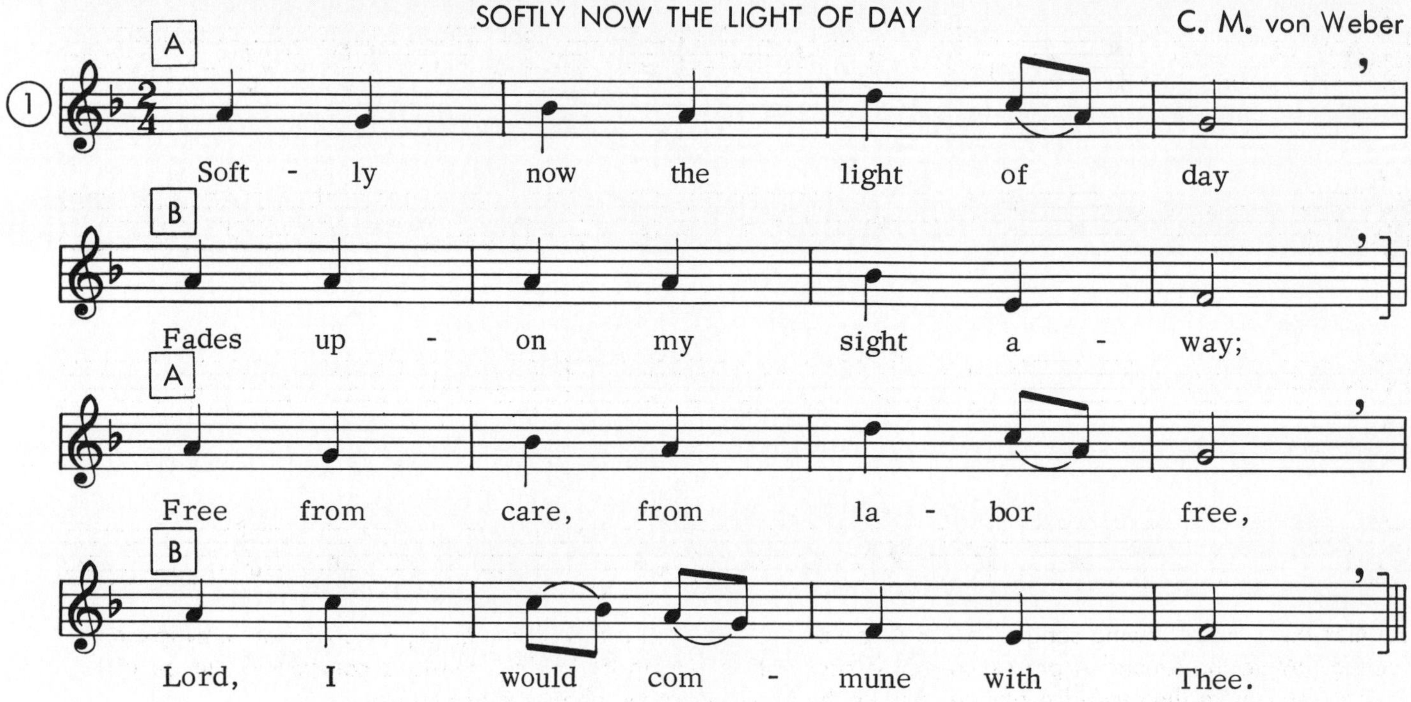
A
1
Soft - ly now the light of day
B
Fades up - on my sight a - way;
A
Free from care, from la - bor free,
B
Lord, I would com - mune with Thee.

In Ex. 2 we have a song which is written in A-A-B-A form. In this case the first, second and fourth phrases are exactly alike but the third phrase is entirely different. In a popular song, this B phrase is called the BRIDGE and is usually the most difficult part to remember.

DECK THE HALL

Old Welsh Air

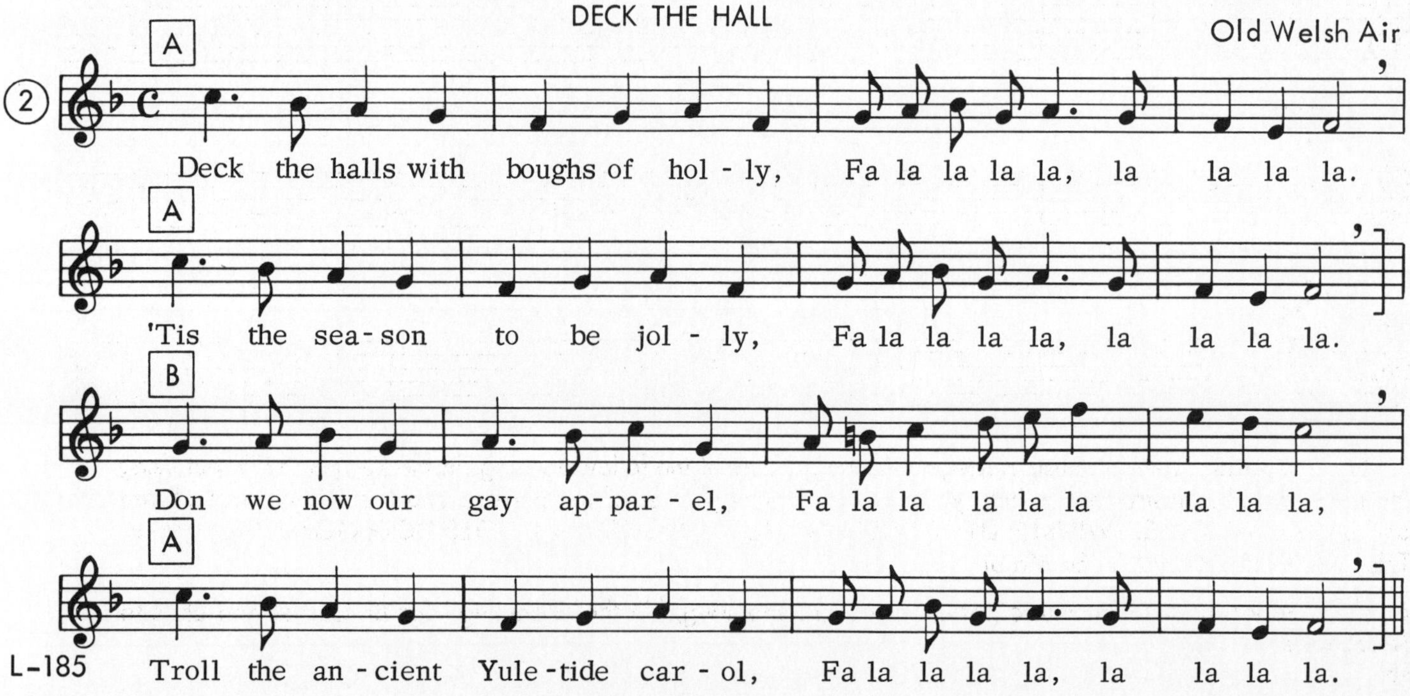
A
2
Deck the halls with boughs of hol - ly, Fa la la la la, la la la la.
A
'Tis the sea- son to be jol - ly, Fa la la la la, la la la la.
B
Don we now our gay ap- par - el, Fa la la la la la la la la,
A
Troll the an - cient Yule-tide car - ol, Fa la la la la, la la la la.

Lesson 66

# STUDENT ASSIGNMENT

Date ________

Grade ________

1. Mark the PHRASES and PERIODS in Ex. 1.

What is the FORM of the Song? ________ ________ ________ ________

How many measures in each PHRASE? ______ In each PERIOD? ______

IN THE GLOAMING

Harrison

(1)

2. Complete the following song in A-A-B-A form. The first A phrase, which is given, ends with an incomplete feeling. Write the second A phrase so that it ends with a feeling of finality. Write a contrasting phrase at B and then repeat the second A phrase to close the song. Mark the phrases and periods.

(2)

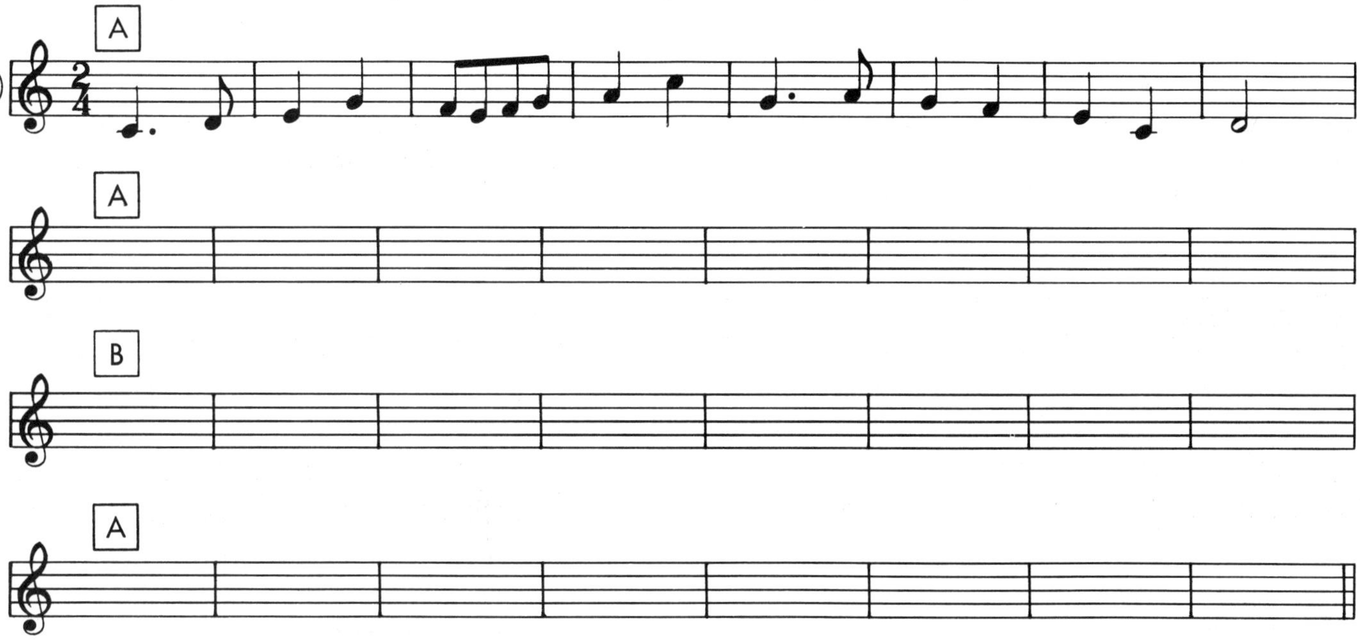


3. On a separate sheet of music paper, write the melody of the following songs in the key given without using the piano or other instrument to help you. Mark the letter names of the phrases and the end of each phrase and period. TWINKLE, TWINKLE, LITTLE STAR in G Major; WHERE IS MY LITTLE DOG GONE? in F Major; THE MARINES' HYMN in E♭ Major.

4. On a separate sheet of music paper, transpose the song, "In the Gloaming" for B♭ Cornet and E♭ Alto Saxophone.

Lesson 67

# CADENCES

A CADENCE is a progression of two or more chords at the end of a phrase or period used to create a feeling of repose.

There are several types of CADENCES:-

1. The PERFECT or AUTHENTIC CADENCE consists of the progression V-I or $V^7$-I, with both chords in root position and the keynote of the tonic chord in the soprano.

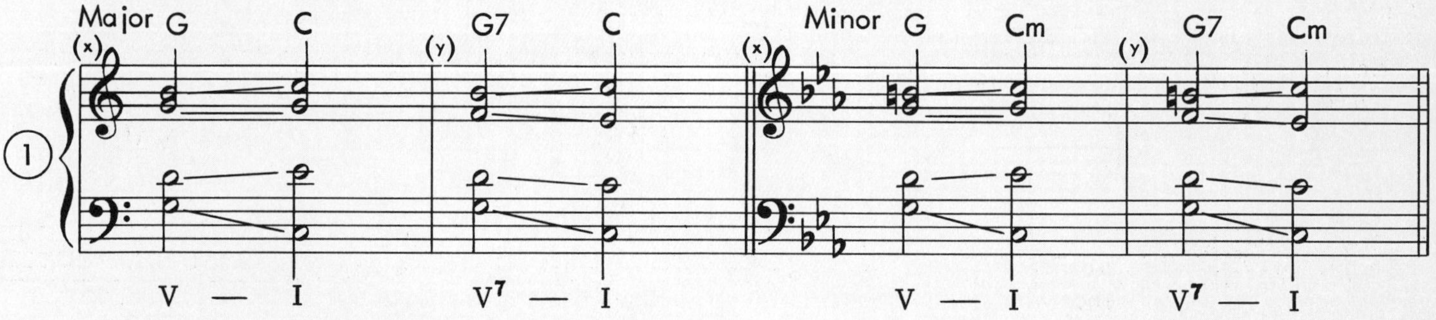


2. The IMPERFECT or INCOMPLETE CADENCE consists of the progression V-I or $V^7$-I, with the 3rd or 5th appearing in the soprano of the final tonic chord.

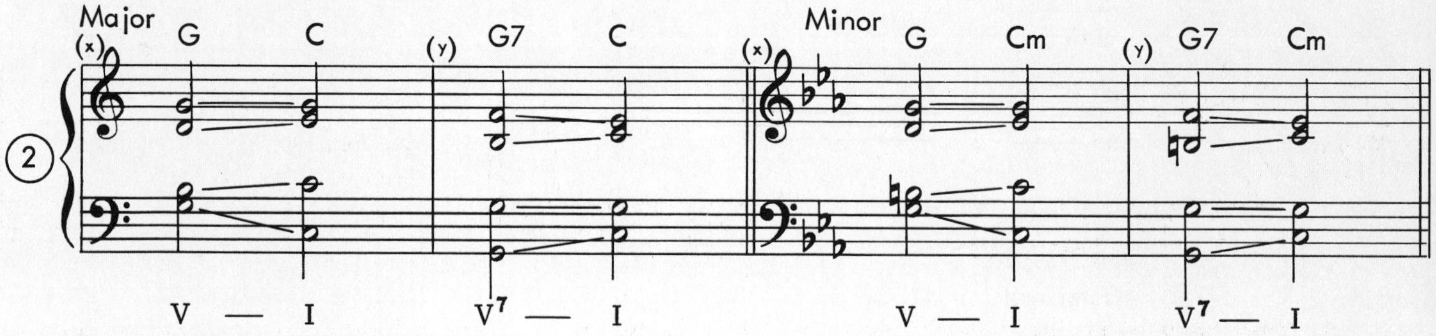


3. The HALF CADENCE ends on the dominant and consists of the progression I-V or IV-V or some other chord followed by the dominant.

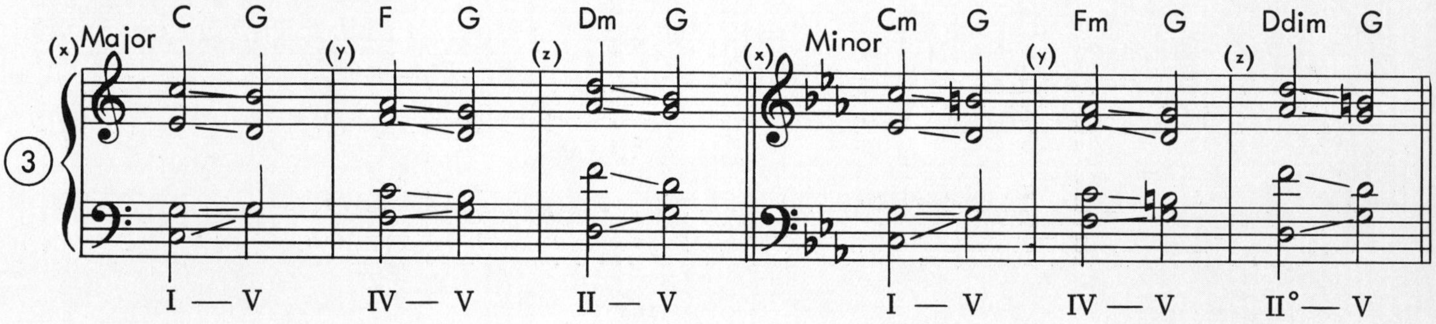


4. The PLAGAL CADENCE consists of the progression IV-I. This is the familiar "Amen" cadence often used at the close of a hymn.

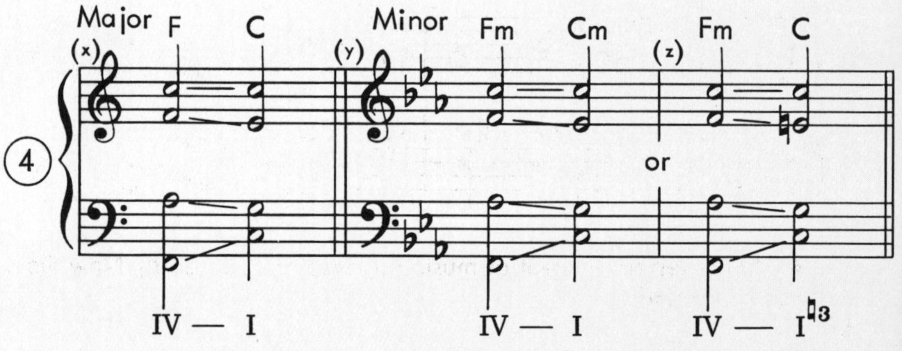

# STUDENT ASSIGNMENT

Date ____________

Grade ____________

1. Write a PERFECT CADENCE in the keys indicated. Write chord symbols below and letter names above.

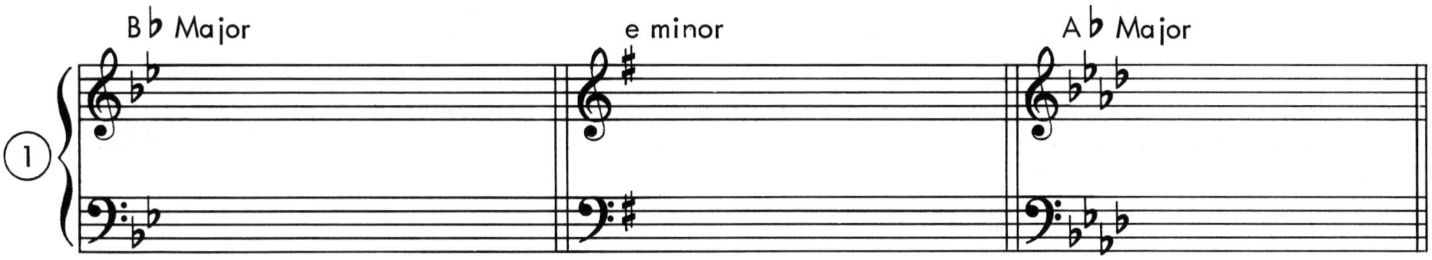


2. In the following cadences write the chord symbols below and the letter names of the chords above. Then write the type of cadence which each one represents on the blank line provided.

Type of cadence

3. In the following song write the chord symbols below and the letter names of the chords above. Mark the phrases and identify the type of cadence at the end of each phrase.

OLD FOLKS AT HOME

Foster

4. On separate music paper arrange the above for Brass Quartet: 1st B♭ Cornet, 2nd B♭ Cornet, Horn in F, Trombone.

Lesson 69

# NON HARMONIC TONES

1. We have previously learned to recognize PASSING NOTES (marked P) and NEIGHBORING NOTES (marked N). (See Master Theory Book 4 - Lesson 5 and Book 5 - Lesson 51.)
Now we will proceed to another type of non harmonic tone which is called a SUSPENSION and is often found at the cadence.
A SUSPENSION is a chord tone which is delayed in its normal resolution so that it becomes a non harmonic tone before resolving to the next chord.
In the 4th measure, the F is held over from the tonic chord and becomes a non harmonic tone before resolving to the 3rd of the dominant.
In the 8th measure, the B♭ is held over from the V7 chord and becomes a non harmonic tone before resolving to the 3rd of the I chord.
The SUSPENSION is marked (S) and includes all three notes; the chord tone, the non harmonic tone and the resolution to a chord tone.

I VI $IV_6$ $V_6$ I II $VII_6$ $I_6$ I Vsus 4 V

I $IV_6$ V $V^7$ VI $II_6$ V $V^7$ I sus 4 I

2. Here are some suspensions in a minor key. (G to G to F♯)

I V $I_6$ V I IV Vsus 4 V $V^7$ I

I $VII_6$ $I_6$ $V_6$ I $IV_6$ Vsus 4 V $V^7$ I

# STUDENT ASSIGNMENT

Date ____________

Grade ____________

Write the name of the key and the chord symbols in Ex. 1-2-3 & 4. The last chord in each example should help you find the name of the key. Mark all SUSPENSIONS with (S).

Ex. 1

Ex. 2

Ex. 3

Ex. 4

Name the types of cadences that were used in Lesson 69.

In Ex. 1 ______________________________, ______________________________

In Ex. 2 ______________________________, ______________________________

Name the types of cadences in the four examples above on this page.

In Ex. 1 ______________________________ Ex. 2 ______________________________

Ex. 3 ______________________________ Ex. 4 ______________________________

The following chorale has a great many, non harmonic tones. Write the chord symbols below and then mark all SUSPENSIONS (S), PASSING NOTES (P) and NEIGHBORING NOTES (N).

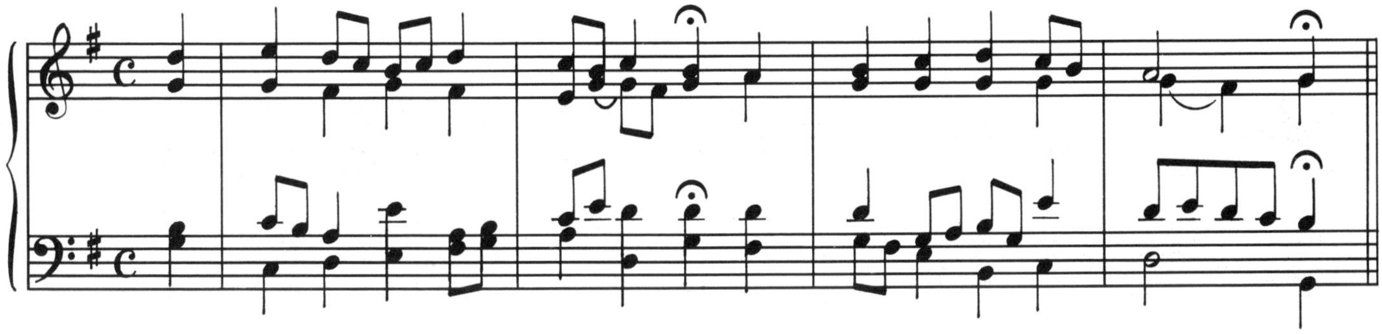

Lesson 71

# NON HARMONIC TONES (continued)

In this lesson we have two more non harmonic tones.
The ANTICIPATION is a tone which precedes the other voices to the next chord. It usually occurs at the cadence and is the exact opposite of the SUSPENSION.
The APPOGGIATURA is a non harmonic tone which occurs on a strong beat and resolves by a step to a chord note either below or above.
We will mark the ANTICIPATION with an (A) and the APPOGGIATURA (Ap).

1. The following example contains all tnree of these non harmonic tones in the soprano.

FATHER, O HEAR ME

Handel

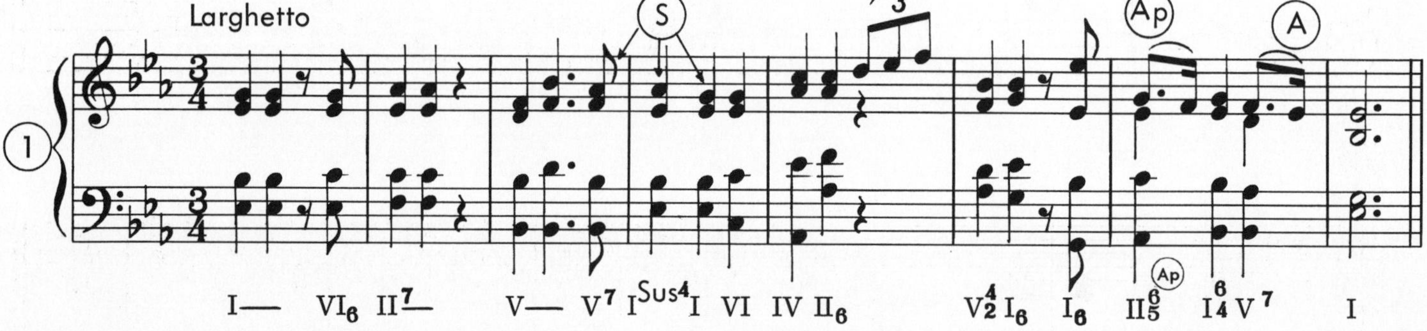


2. In this next excerpt from Handel, we have two SUSPENSIONS (one of which resolves upward) and an ANTICIPATION.

SARABANDE

Largo

Handel

3. Play the following on the piano for interesting examples of the APPOGGIATURA and SUSPENSION. (Notice the two treble clef signs.)

THE NEW DOLL

Allegro

Tschaikowsky

# STUDENT ASSIGNMENT

Date ____________

Grade ____________

Analyze the harmony in Ex. 1-2-3-4 and write the chord symbols below in each case. Mark all the non harmonic tones:- PASSING NOTES (P), NEIGHBORING NOTES (N), SUSPENSION (S), ANTICIPATION (A) and APPOGGIATURA (Ap). Play the examples on the piano.

(1) (2)

(3) (4)

In the excerpt from this famous Bach Chorale, Ex. 5, you should find at least one example of each of the non harmonic tones we have studied. Write the chord symbols below and mark all of the non harmonic tones.

COME SWEET DEATH

J.S.Bach

(5)

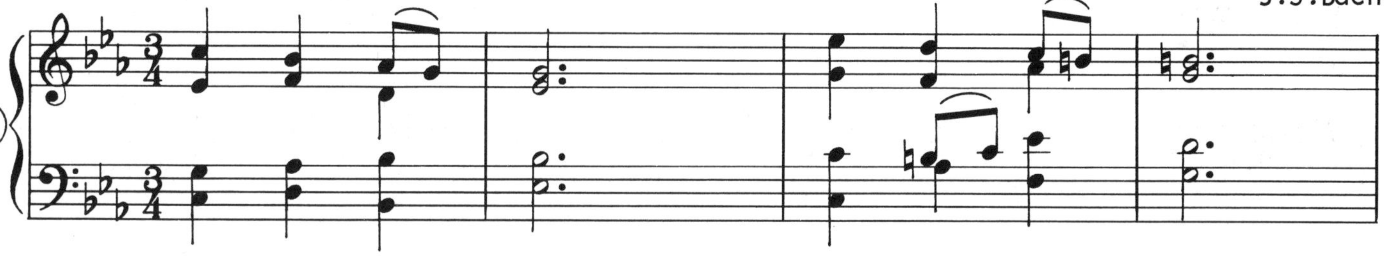

On a separate sheet of music paper, arrange the portion of "Father, O Hear Me" in lesson 71, for Saxophone Quartet consisting of 1st Eb Alto, 2nd Eb Alto, Bb Tenor and Eb Baritone Saxophones.

On another separate sheet of music paper, arrange the portion of "Come Sweet Death" for Clarinet Quartet consisting of 1st Bb Clarinet, 2nd Bb Clarinet, Eb Alto Clarinet and Bb Bass Clarinet.

# SIMPLE MODULATION

MODULATION is the process of moving from one key to another. The most common type of modulation is that which is made to a closely related key, thru a PIVOT CHORD which is found in both keys.

In Ex. 1 the PIVOT CHORD (marked X) serves as the tonic in the key of F and the subdominant in the key of C.

Ex. 2 shows a modulation to the dominant of the relative major key thru the PIVOT CHORD (X).

In both examples a cadence serves to establish the new key.

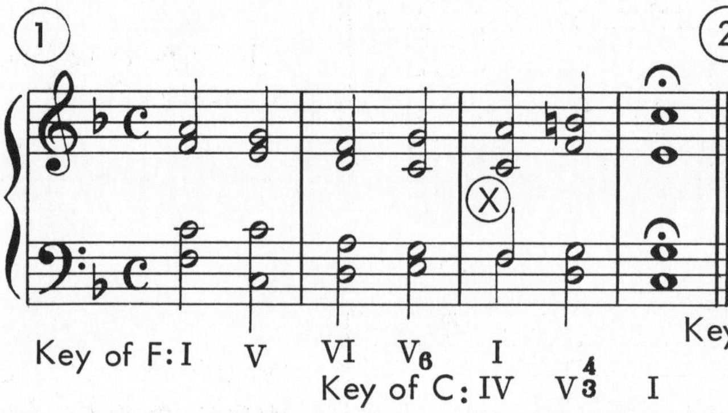


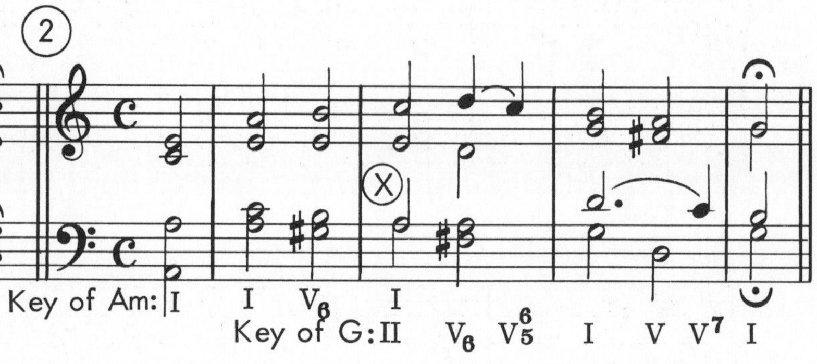


Ex. 3 modulates from F major to C major and then to B♭ major. Notice the PIVOT CHORDS in each case and the cadence which establishes the new key. Also notice the passing note and the suspension which are indicated.

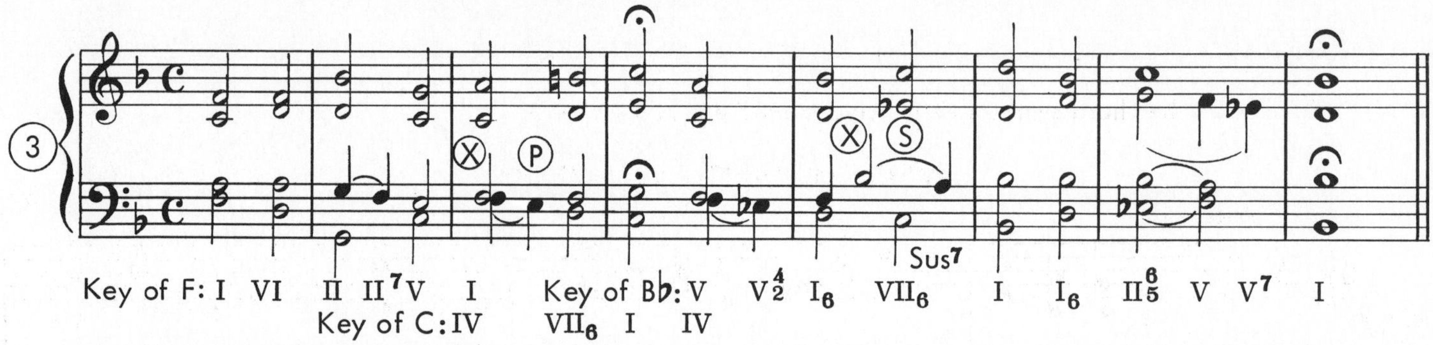


In this classic composition for piano, Ex. 4, we will write only the letter names of the chords since the arpeggios which appear in the left hand are not considered as inversions. However the modulation at the cadence is perfectly clear.

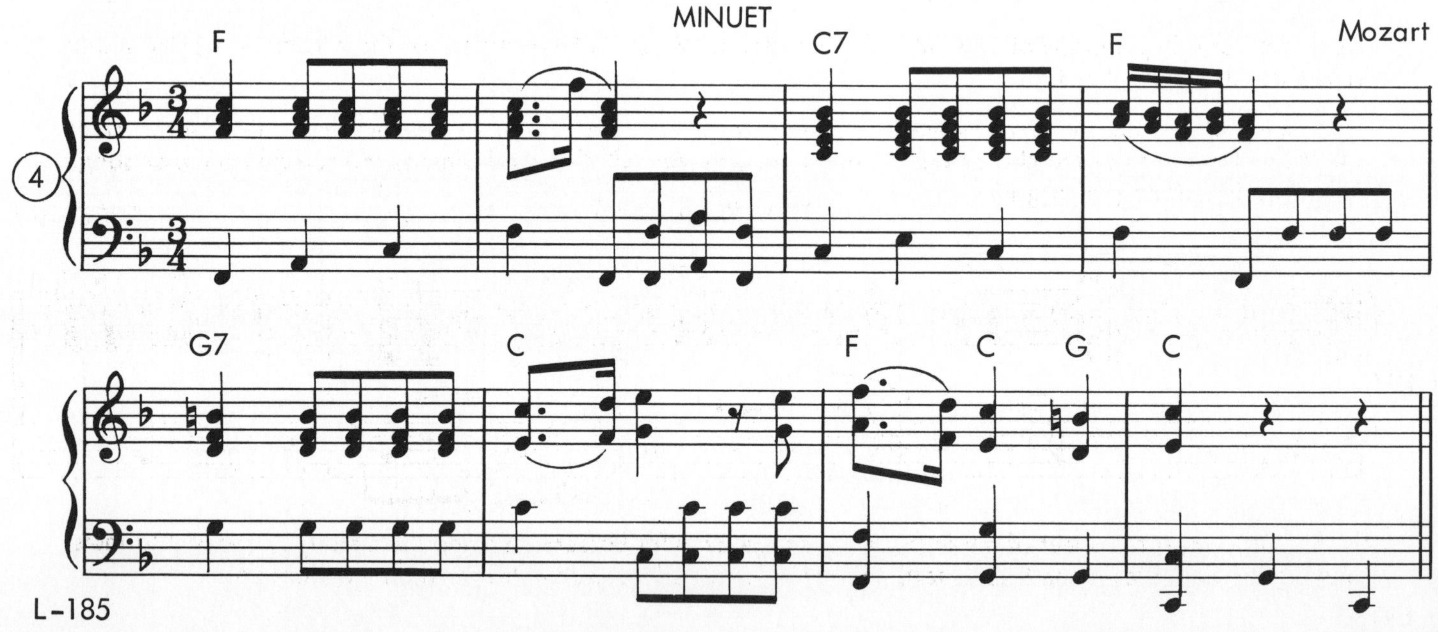

Lesson 74

# STUDENT ASSIGNMENT

Date __________

Grade __________

In Ex. 1 and 2 analyze the harmony and write the chord symbols below. Notice the modulation and show both keys as in lesson 71. Mark the PIVOT CHORD with an (X).

(1)

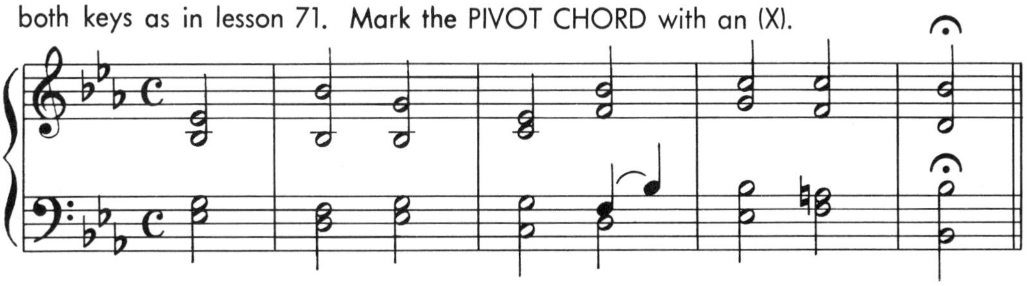

What type of cadence do we have in Ex. 1?

________________

(2)

What is the relation of the second key in Ex. 2 to the first key?

________________

In Ex. 3 write the chord symbols below and mark the PIVOT CHORD.

WHEN MORNING GILDS THE SKIES

Barnby

(3)

Ex. 4 is a very simple modulation written for the piano. Write the letter names of the chords above the music and mark the pivot chord.

Since the melody is in the lowest voice, we do not consider these arpeggios as inversions. It is sufficient to use the letter names of the chords only. This is the way you will find the harmony indicated in popular songs published for piano and organ.

THE MERRY FARMER

Schumann

(4)

Ex. 5. On a separate sheet of music paper, arrange Ex. 4 for Bassoon (playing the melody), three B♭ Clarinets (playing the 8th notes in the treble staff) and three C Flutes (one octave higher than the clarinets).

## Lesson 75

# MILITARY MARCHES

Anyone who has played in a band is familiar with the military march. Most marches are quite similar in their form and harmonic construction.

The usual form of a march is as follows:-

- INTRODUCTION — 4 to 8 measures
- FIRST STRAIN — 16 measures, repeated
- SECOND STRAIN — 16 measures, repeated
- TRIO — 32 measures, repeated — sometimes followed by an Interlude strain with a return to the Trio.

The INTRODUCTION often contains a unison passage or some fanfare type figures for the brass.

The FIRST STRAIN usually starts on the tonic chord and consists of two, eight measure phrases forming a complete period. The second one of these phrases often modulates to the dominant as in this well known march.

SALUTATION

R.F.Seitz

Lesson 76

# STUDENT ASSIGNMENT

| | |
|---|---|
| Date | ________ |
| Grade | ________ |

1. In Lesson 75, mark the passing notes (P) and the neighboring notes (N) in the first strain of "Salutation."

2. What type of cadence is used at the end of this first strain? ______________________

3. Notice the bass part at (x) and (y). The bass usually alternates between the root and 5th of the tonic chord, in that order, as at (x). In the dominant seventh chord, the bass almost always alternates between the 5th and root in that order as at (y).

(x)

(y)

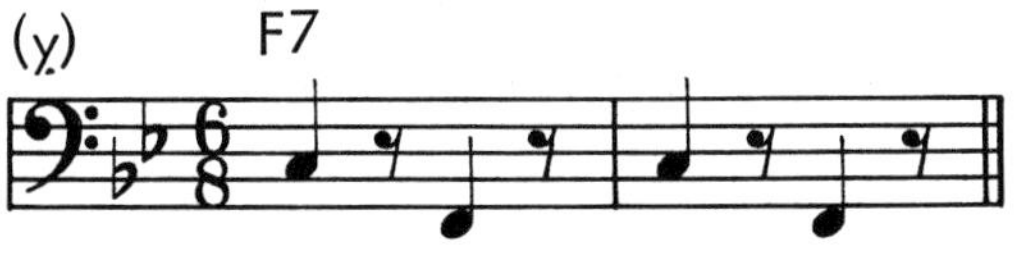


(z)

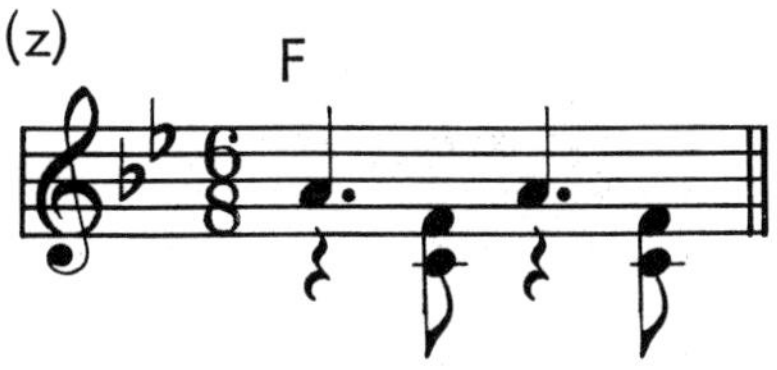


4. At (z) we modulate to the key of F major thru a pivot chord. This chord is the V in the original key of B♭ and the I in the new key of F.

5. Using the same harmonic scheme that we had in "Salutation," write an original INTRODUCTION and FIRST STRAIN of a march.

(Introduction)

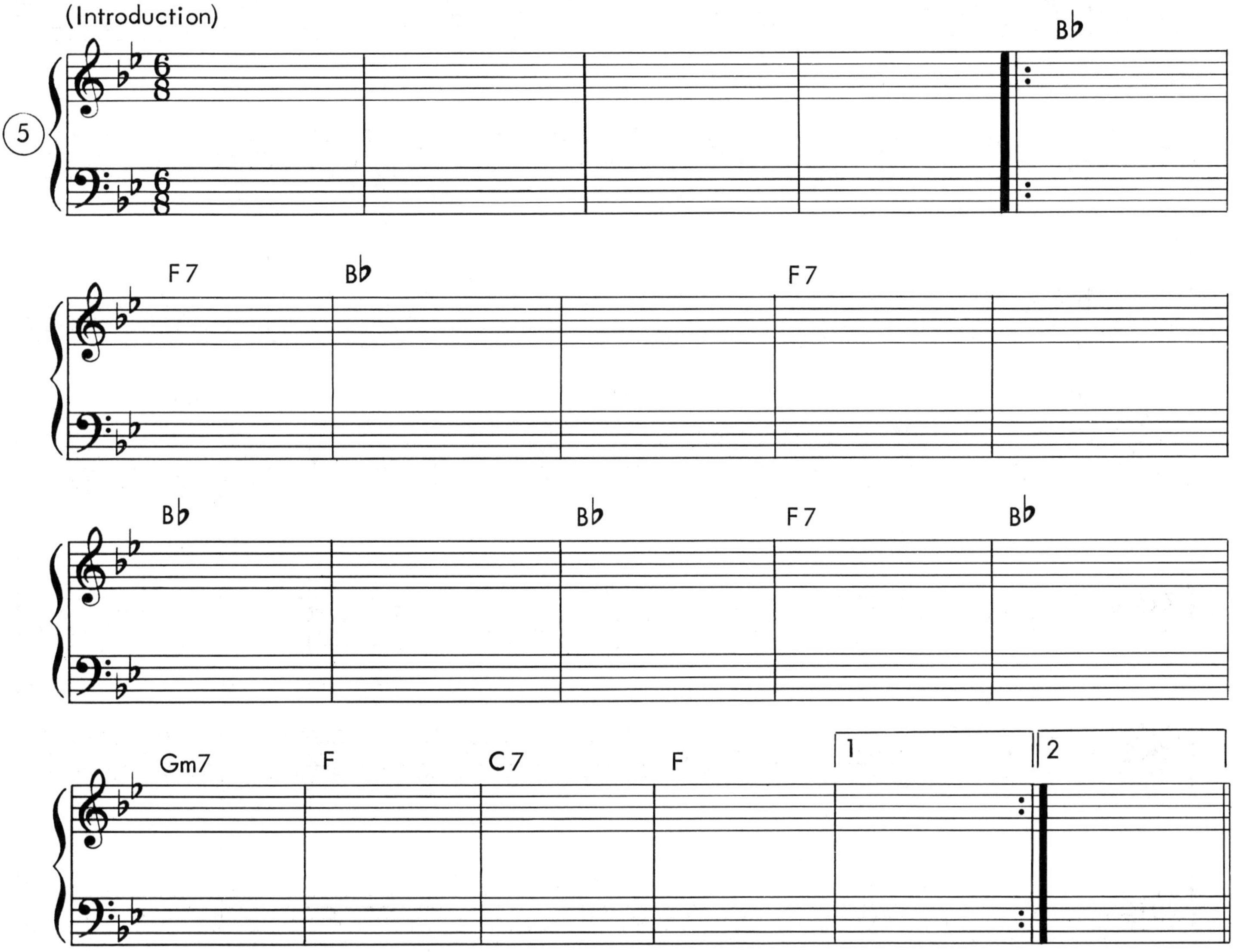

Lesson 77

# MILITARY MARCHES (continued)

After the modulation to the dominant in the first strain, the second strain invariably starts on the $V^7$ chord of the original key. It is quite common to make a diminuendo in the fourth measure and play the next four bars softly for contrast.

The second phrase of this strain returns to a forte or fortissimo and then passes thru some form of subdominant harmony before concluding with the tonic of the original key.

In the second strain of "Salutation" (below), notice the scale movement in the bass part which adds excitement to this ***ff*** passage. The bass returns to a regular rhythmic part when the band drops to ***p*** in the fifth measure.

At (x) the accent gives greater emphasis to the subdominant chord with a lowered third (E♭ minor) which is the climax of this strain. At (y) we have the standard approach to a perfect cadence thru $I^6_4 - V^7 - I$.

SALUTATION (2nd Strain)

R. F. Seitz

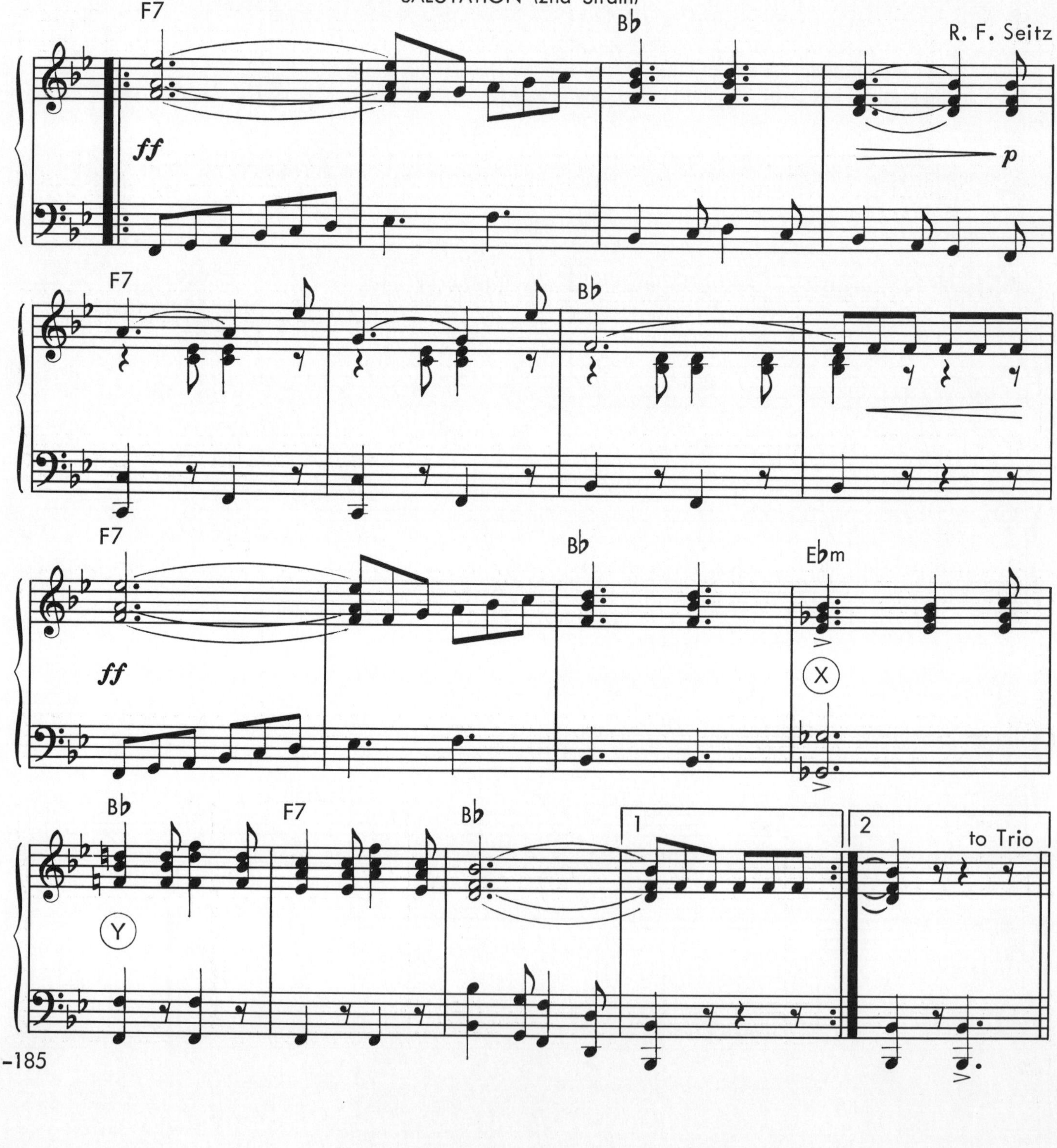

# STUDENT ASSIGNMENT

Date ____________

Grade ____________

1. In Lesson 77, mark the passing notes (P) in the second strain of "Salutation."

2. What type of cadence is used at the end of the second strain? ______________________________
Study the movement of the bass part. Whenever a number of passing notes appear, the first note of the measure (strong beat) is almost always on a chord tone. See the marches of Sousa, King, Fillmore and Goldman for examples of good bass parts. This is extremely important.

3. Using the same harmonic scheme that we had in the second strain of "Salutation," write a SECOND STRAIN for your march.

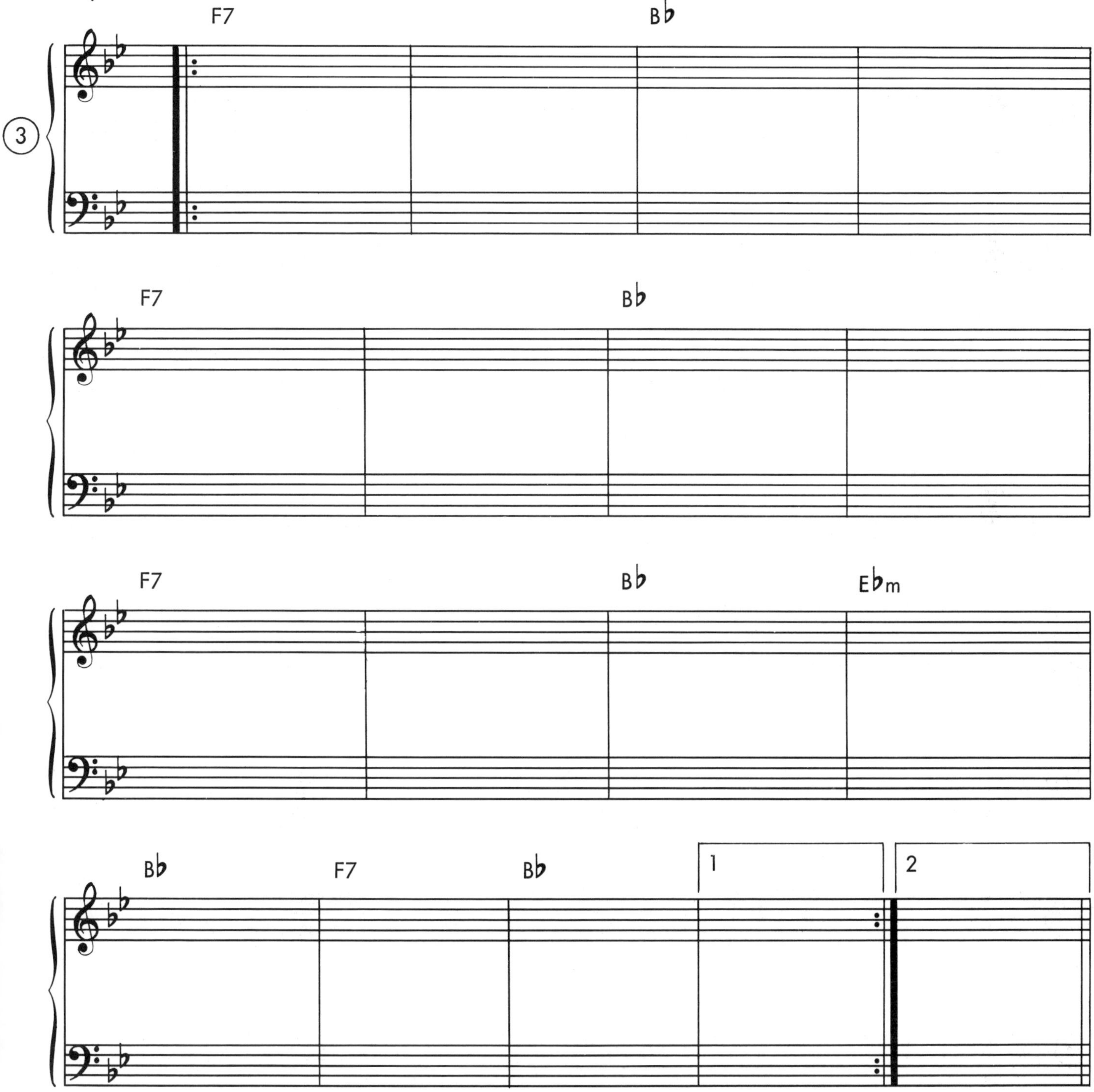

# MILITARY MARCHES (continued)

The TRIO of a march is almost always written in the key of the subdominant, therefore we add one flat or subtract one sharp from the key signature, as the case may be.

SALUTATION (Trio)

R.F.Seitz

TRIO

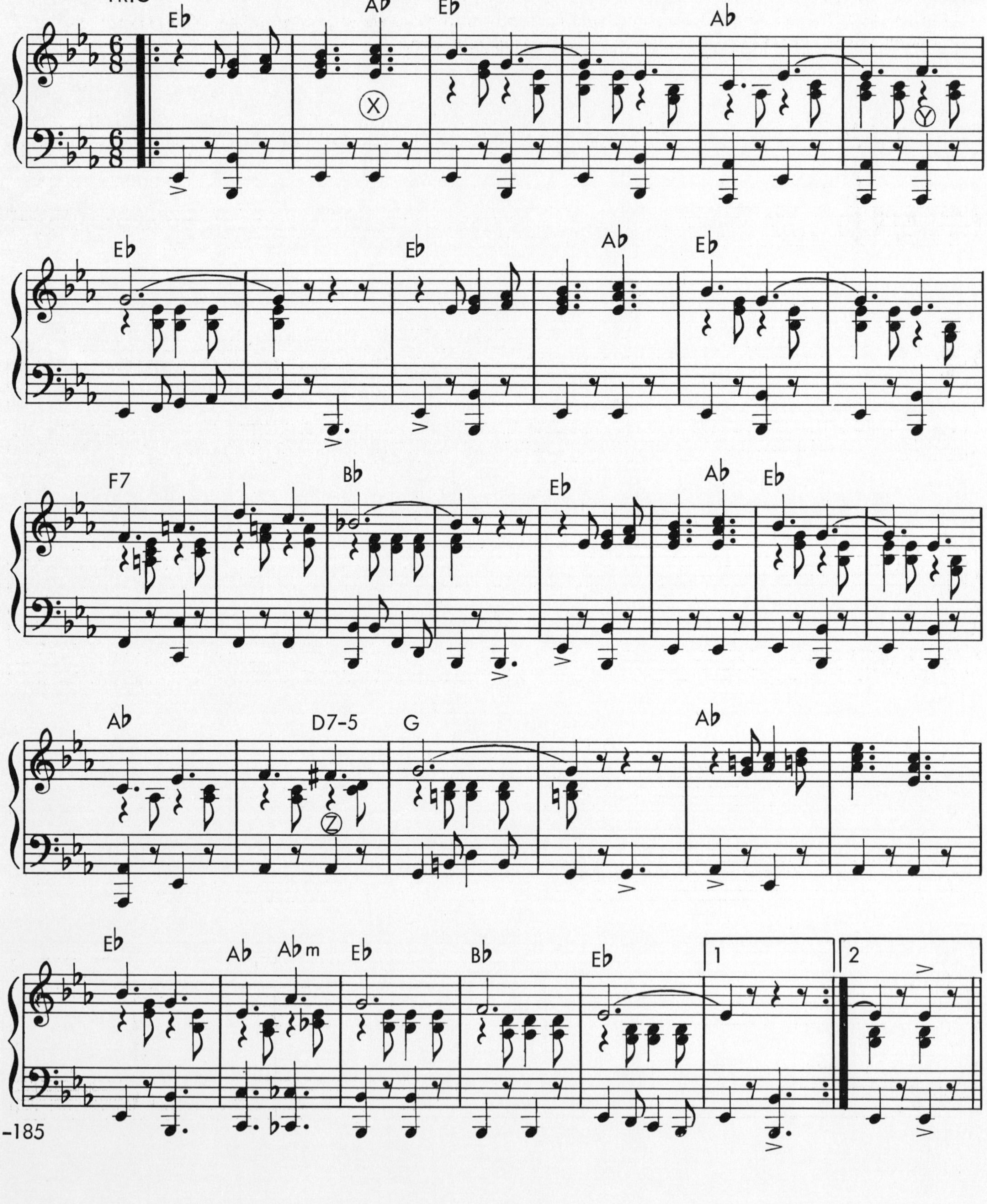

# STUDENT ASSIGNMENT

Date ________

Grade ________

In Lesson 79 at (x) we keep the E♭ in the bass as a common tone between the tonic (E♭) and subdominant (A♭) chords. At (y) the F in the melody may be considered as a passing tone or as the added sixth of an A♭ chord. At (z) we modulate briefly to the key of G major thru the D7 with a lowered 5th.
Now, write a TRIO of 32 measures in the key of E♭ major, to complete your own march. You may follow the harmonic scheme in the Trio of "Salutation" or develop your own.

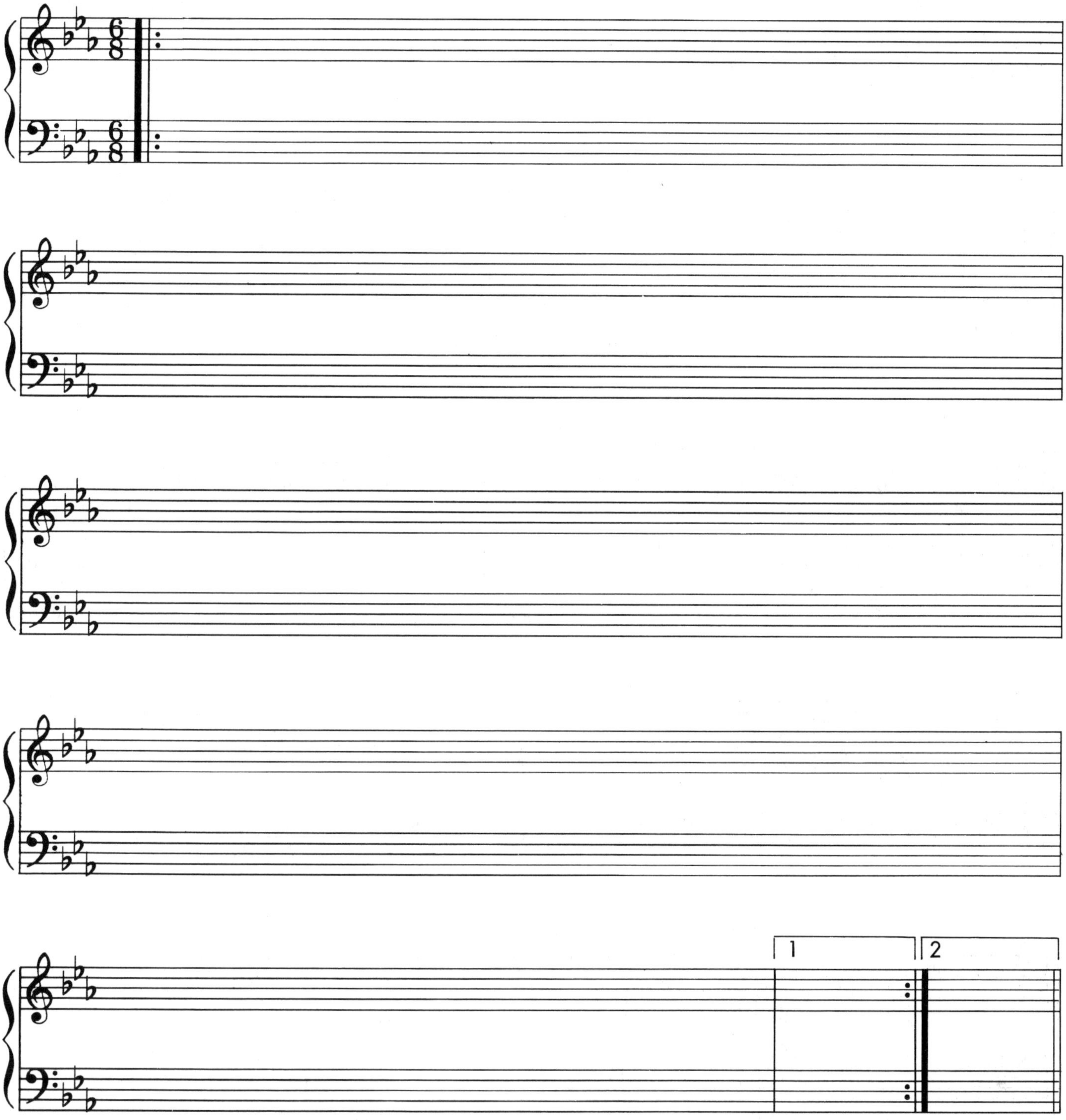

# THE DOMINANT NINTH CHORD

In major keys, a DOMINANT NINTH CHORD consists of a root, major 3rd, perfect 5th, minor 7th and major 9th. It is marked V9 and the figure 9 is added to the letter name of the chord (G9).

In minor keys, a DOMINANT NINTH CHORD consist of a root, major 3rd, perfect 5th, minor 7th and MINOR 9th. It is marked V-9 and the minus 9 is added to the letter name of the chord (G-9).

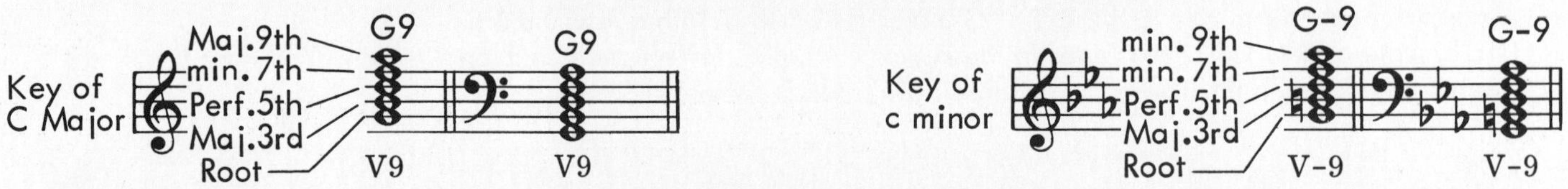


Since there are five notes in the V9 chord, one of these must be omitted in writing four part choral arrangements. We usually omit the 5th.

## STUDENT ASSIGNMENT

Date ________ Grade ________

1. Fill in the missing notes in the examples below so that each chord consists of four notes — root, 3rd, 7th, 9th.

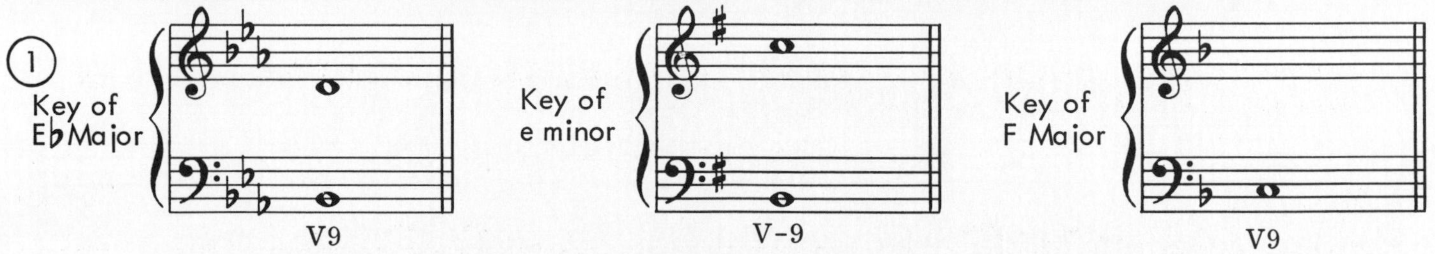


2. On a separate sheet of music paper, arrange "In the Evening By the Moonlight" for a Brass Quartet of two Bb Trumpets and two Trombones.

IN THE EVENING BY THE MOONLIGHT

# STUDENT ASSIGNMENT

| | |
|---|---|
| Date | ________ |
| Grade | ________ |

1. Write the DOMINANT NINTH CHORD in close position, in the keys indicated below. Check the clef signs carefully and mark the letter name above each chord.

Key of Bb Major 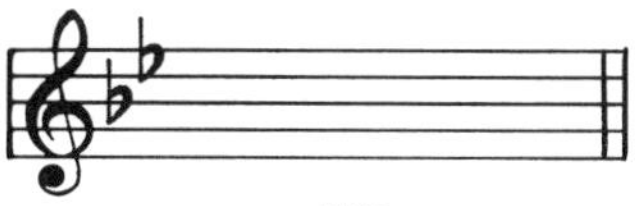 V9

Key of g minor 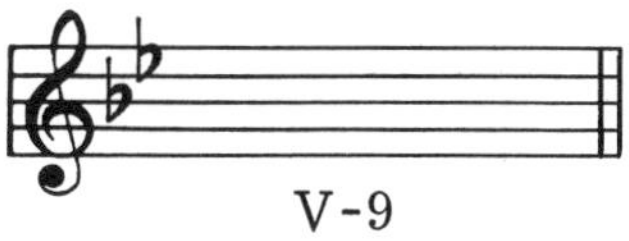 V-9

Key of G Major 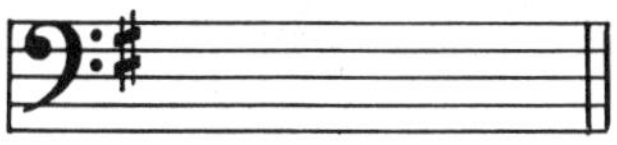 V9

Key of d minor 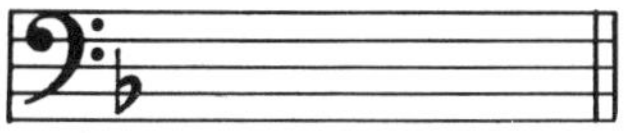 V-9

Key of D Major 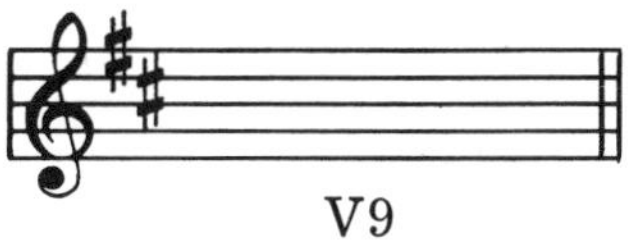 V9

Key of Eb Major 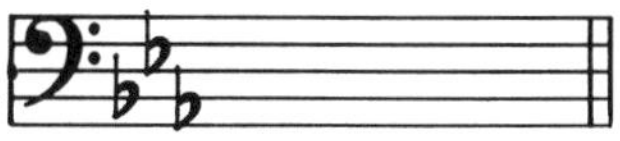 V9

2. Write the letter names above the chords in the following song. Since this is written for piano, you will notice that all five notes appear in the V9 chords.

FRANKIE and JOHNNY

Blues Tempo (Ballad)

3. On a separate sheet of manuscript paper, arrange "Frankie and Johnny" for five Saxophones:- two Eb Altos, two Bb Tenors and Eb Baritone. Use all five notes in the V9 chords. In triads, either double one of the upper voices or experiment with an added sixth.* Write the upper notes of the bass part for the Baritone Saxophone.

Lesson 83

# THE DIMINISHED SEVENTH CHORD

The DIMINISHED SEVENTH CHORD is built on the leading tone of the minor scale. It consists of a root, minor 3rd, diminished 5th and diminished 7th. It is marked $VII^{\circ 7}$ and $dim^7$ is added to the letter name of the chord ($Gdim^7$).

This same chord may be used in major keys by lowering the 7th of the chord a half step.

(1)

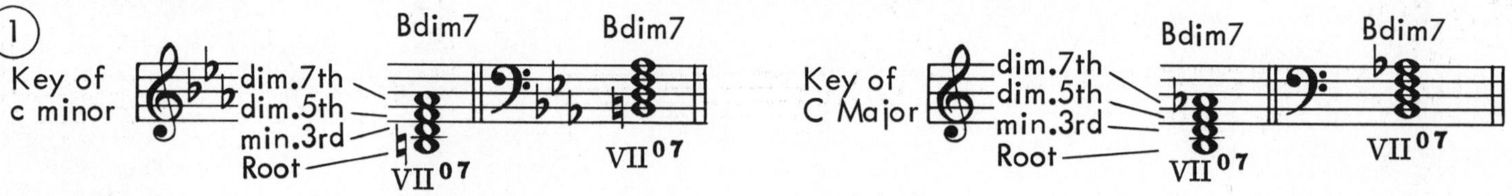


Since the DIMINISHED SEVENTH CHORD actually consists of a series of minor 3rds, there are only three such chords. In the examples below the two chords at (x) contain the same four notes although they are in a different position. This is also true of the chords at (y) and (z).

To find the letter name of the $VII^{\circ 7}$ chord, think of these four notes as they would appear in a series of minor thirds and name the chord for the lowest note. For example at (x) the chord would be spelled G#, B, D, F so we label it as a G#dim7.

(2)

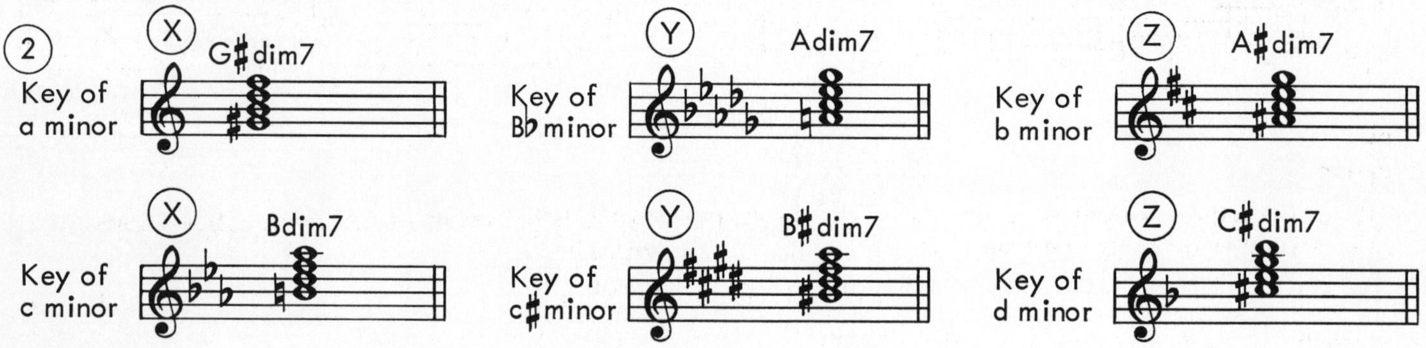


Study the diminished seventh chords in Examples 3 and 4.

I HEARD THE BELLS ON CHRISTMAS DAY

Calkin

(3)

O LITTLE TOWN OF BETHLEHEM

Redner

(4)

Lesson 84

# STUDENT ASSIGNMENT

| | |
|---|---|
| Date | ________ |
| Grade | ________ |

1. Write the DIMINISHED SEVENTH CHORDS in close position, in the keys indicated. Watch the clef signs. Remember to lower the 7th of the $VII^{\circ 7}$ in major keys and raise the root (leading tone) in minor keys. Write the letter name of the chord above in each case.

(1)

Key of d minor

Key of D Major

Key of B♭ Major

Key of G Major
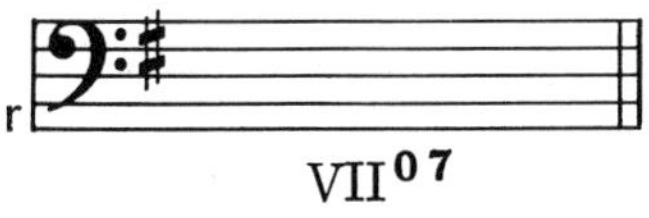


Key of a minor
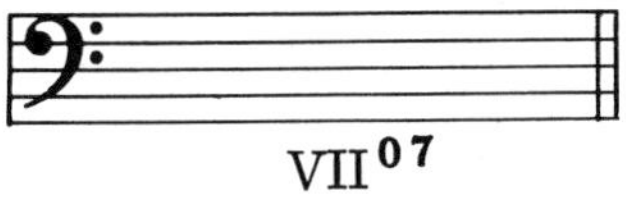


Key of A Major
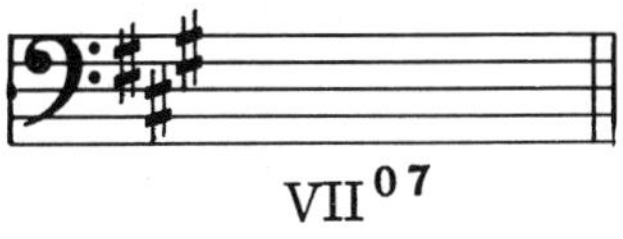


2. Fill in the missing notes of these DIMINISHED SEVENTH CHORDS in open position. Remember that the letter name of the chord represents the lowest note in these examples.

(2)

Key of c minor

Bdim7

Key of D Major

C♯dim7

Key of g minor

F♯dim7

3. Write the letter names of the chords above the treble staff in Ex. 3. Try to form a mental picture of each $VII^{\circ 7}$ chord as it would appear in a series of minor thirds, then name the chord for the lowest note.

SOFTLY NOW THE LIGHT OF DAY

C.M. von Weber

(3)
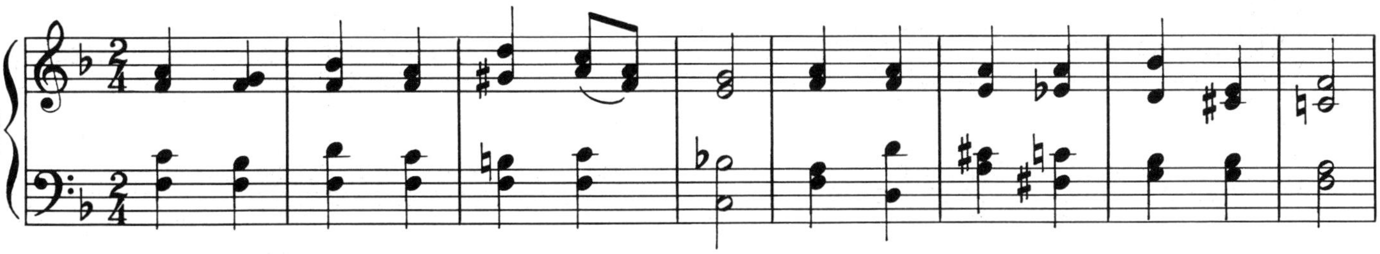

4. On a separate sheet of music paper, arrange "Softly Now the Light of Day" for Oboe, B♭ Clarinet, French Horn in F and Bassoon.

Lesson 85

# THE STRING SECTION

Music for the Violin is written in the G or Treble Clef and the open strings sound G - D - A - E.

Music for the Viola is written in the C or Alto Clef (the third line is middle C) and the open strings sound C - G - D - A.

Music for the Cello is written in the F or Bass Clef and the open strings sound an octave below the Viola C - G - D - A.

Music for the String Bass (Double Bass or Contrabass) is written in the F or Bass Clef. The String Bass sounds one octave below the written note and the four strings are:- E - A - D - G.

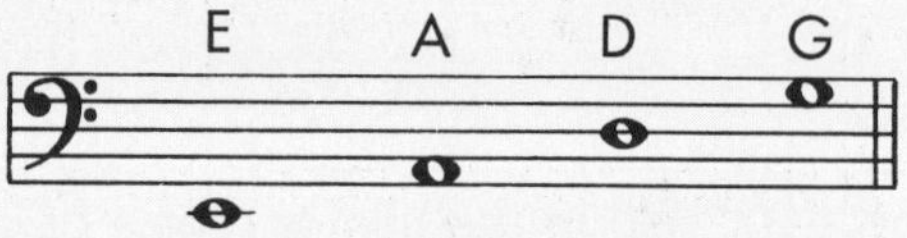


Because of the tuning of the open strings, the music for these instruments is often written in keys that have one or more sharps in the signature.

Here are the first four bars of a well known hymn as it appears in the hymnal and then arranged for the string section. Notice that the Cello and String Bass play the Bass part in octaves, although the notation is exactly alike for both instruments.

HARK THE HERALD ANGELS SING

Mendelssohn

Lesson 86

# STUDENT ASSIGNMENT

Date ____________

Grade ____________

In the beautiful folk song below, you will find most of the chords we have studied in this book. Write in the letter names of the chords and mark all non harmonic tones. Notice the AUGMENTED FIFTH chords which have already been marked. This consists of a root, major third and augmented fifth.

Now take some manuscript paper and make a five line score of this song for strings as is shown in lesson 85. Write the highest note for 1st violin, next for 2nd violin, next for viola, then use cello and bass on the bass part. You will need to double one of the other voices when only three notes are shown. Copy off the parts on separate sheets and try to have this played.

VIENNESE REFRAIN

Folk Song

Lesson 87

# KEY RELATION

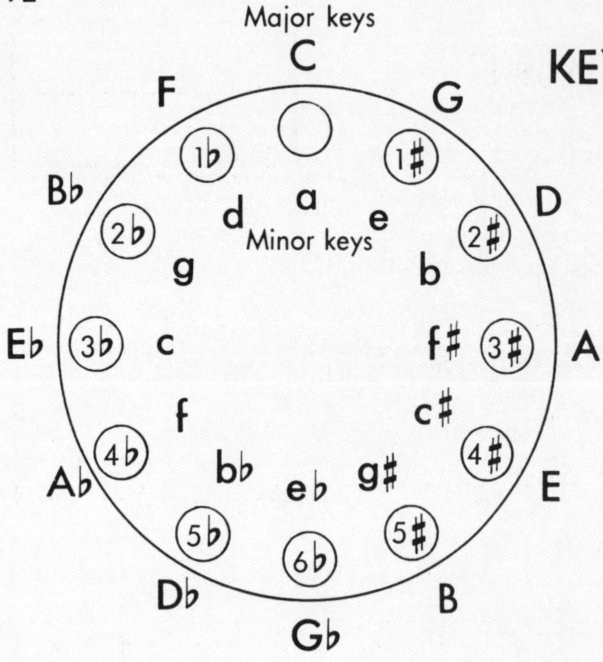


In Master Theory Book 2 we studied the relation of keys thru the circle of fifths. You will find, upon examination, that many compositions, both classical and popular, progress thru a series of V7 chords without actually modulating away from the original key. Such chords are called CONSECUTIVE DOMINANT SEVENTHS. Here are two examples.

LIEBESTRAUME

Liszt

The bridge passage from "GYPSY LOVE SONG"

Victor Herbert

# STUDENT ASSIGNMENT

Date ________

Grade ________

1. The following sequence goes around the circle of MAJOR KEYS thru the tonic and dominant seventh chords. Fill in the missing notes in the manner of the first two measures and write the letter names of the chords above.

2. Here is the same series of I, V7 chords thru the circle of MINOR KEYS. Check the minor and major 3rds carefully and fill in the missing notes. Write the letter names of the chords above.

3. Complete this chromatic progression of diminished seventh chords by writing a series of minor thirds above the given notes. Notice that there are only three different $VII^{\circ 7}$ chords, after which they repeat the same notes in a different position and different notation. Write the letter names of the chords above.

Lesson 89

| Date ______ |
|---|
| Grade ______ |

# STUDENT TEST

Lessons 63-65 1. Mark the phrases and periods in the following song.

2. Analyze the form of the song and mark each phrase A or B.

3. What is the form of this song? ______ ______ ______ ______

4. How many measures in each phrase? ______ In each period? ______

OH! SUSANNA

Foster

Lesson 67 1. Write the chord symbols below the following cadences.

2. Write the name of each cadence on the blank above the music.

3. Name the key in which each cadence is written.

(w) ______ (x) ______ (y) ______ (z) ______

(w) ______ (x) ______ (y) ______ (z) ______

Lessons 69-71 1. There is only one non harmonic tone in each of these examples. Write the name of each non harmonic tone in the blank provided.

(v) ______ (w) ______ (x) ______ (y) ______ (z) ______

2. Write the chord symbols below the following example and mark all non harmonic tones. Passing notes (P) Neighboring notes (N) Suspension (S) Anticipation (A) Appoggiatura (Ap).

# STUDENT TEST

Lesson 73 1. Analyze the harmony in the following modulations. Write the chord symbols below and the letter names of the chords above. Locate the pivot chord and show what relation it has to both keys thru the chord symbols.

2. Name the relation of the two keys in each modulation.

(x) modulates to the ________________ (y) modulates to the ____________________

Lessons 75-79 1. The following example is the first strain of a march. Write the letter names of the chords above the treble staff.

2. What is the original key of the march? ______________________________

3. To what key does this strain modulate? ______________________________

MARCH

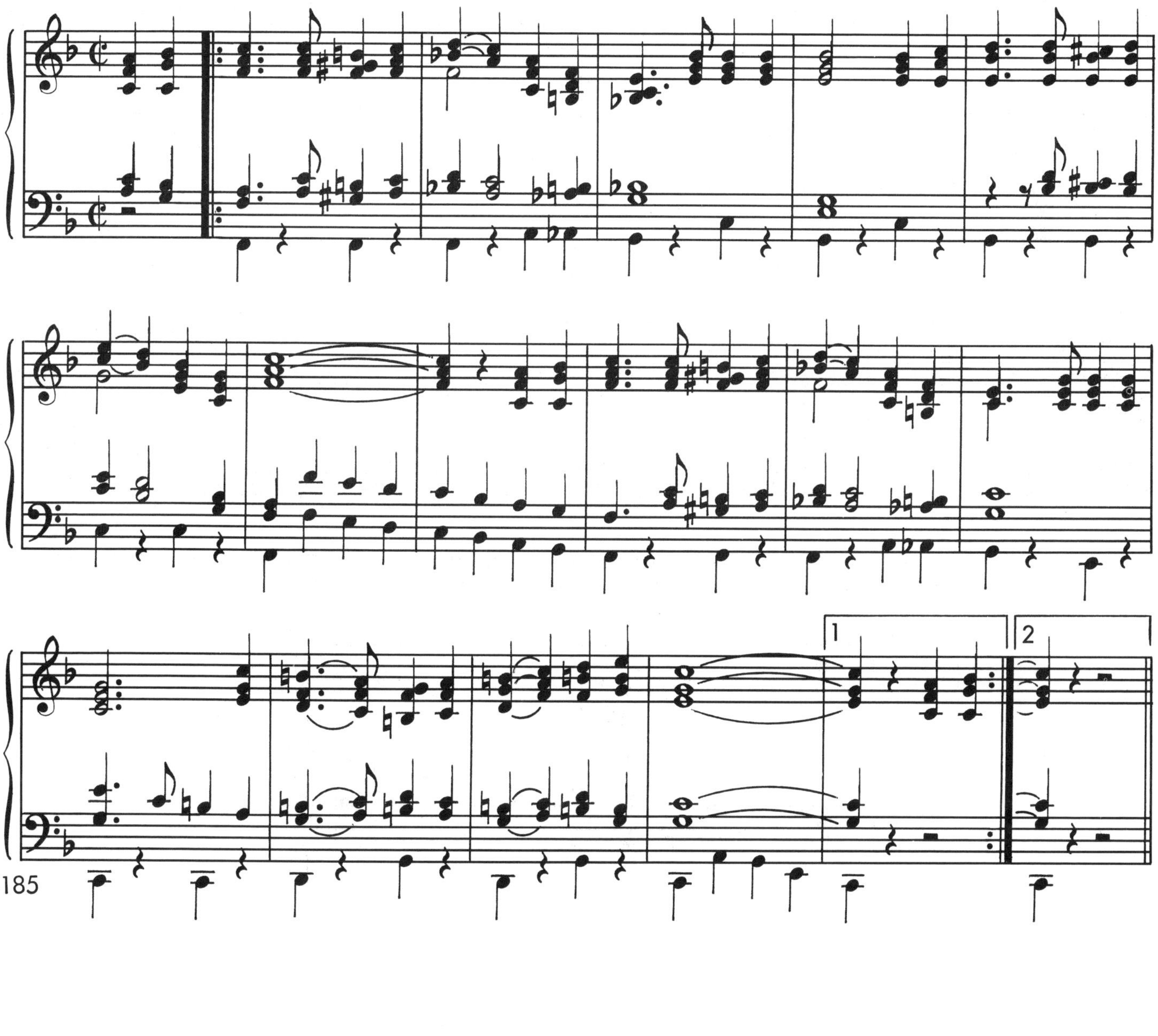

Lesson 90

# STUDENT TEST

| | |
|---|---|
| Date | ________ |
| Grade | ________ |

Lesson 81 1. Write a dominant ninth chord($V9$) in close position, in the keys indicated below. Write the letter name of each chord above.

Key of C Major 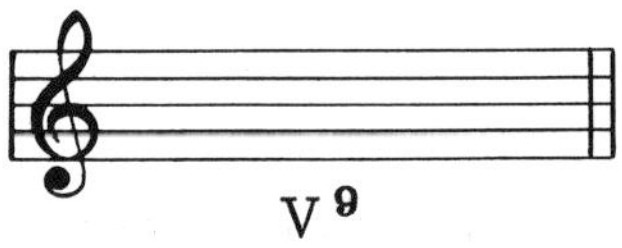 $V^9$

Key of e minor 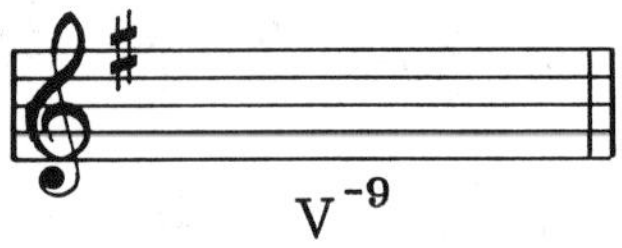 $V^{-9}$

Key of D♭Major  $V^9$

Lesson 83 1. Write a diminished seventh chord $VII^{o7}$ in close position, in the keys indicated below. Write the letter name of each chord above.

Key of d minor 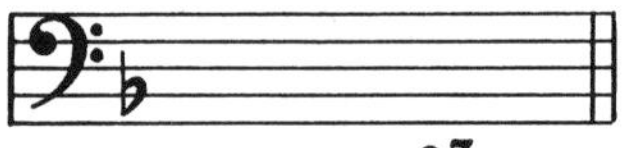 $VII^{07}$

Key of A♭Major  $VII^{07}$

Key of b minor 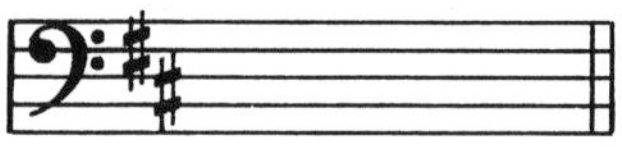 $VII^{07}$

Lesson 87 1. Write the letter names of the chords above the following song. On separate music paper, arrange "On the Banks of the Wabash" for Saxophone Quartet — 1st E♭ Alto, 2nd E♭ Alto, B♭ Tenor and E♭ Baritone Saxophones. Write each instrument in the proper transposed key and each on a separate line.

ON THE BANKS OF THE WABASH

Paul Dresser

Slowly